T0031514

Who Is
Jeff Kinney?

by Patrick Kinney

illustrated by John Hinderliter

Penguin Workshop

To Mom and Dad—PK

For Caroline, a stylish adventurer, who biked more of the
Northern Rail Trail than any of her siblings—JH

PENGUIN WORKSHOP
An Imprint of Penguin Random House LLC, New York

Diary of a Wimpy Kid (2007), *Diary of a Wimpy Kid: Rodrick Rules* (2008),
Diary of a Wimpy Kid: The Last Straw (2009), and *Diary of a Wimpy Kid: The Long Haul*
(2014) are published by Amulet, an imprint of ABRAMS. *Diário de um Banana* (2007) is
published under license by Vergara & Riba. Permission has been granted by Jeff Kinney to
render images of his characters in this biography.

Library of Congress Control Number: 2015019203

ISBN 9780448486772

Contents

Who Is
Jeff Kinney?

In Patricia and Brian Kinney's home in Virginia, there is a framed newspaper article hanging on the wall. The headline reads: "Igdoof Takes On the Real World." There is a photo of their son Jeff, twenty-two years old, grinning next to a drawing of a bug-eyed cartoon character. That character was Igdoof. In college, Jeff wrote and illustrated a popular comic strip about him. The article predicted that Jeff would have no trouble becoming a professional cartoonist. That was his dream.

But after several years of disappointment, Jeff wasn't so sure. When he came home to visit his parents, he'd look at the article and frown. He wondered if his dream would ever come true.

In college, Jeff had been a celebrity. Fans of *Igdoof* asked Jeff for his autograph. They wore T-shirts with characters from his comic strip on them.

Besides Igdoof, there was a green bean named Pooshfa. Another was Jerome, a man with incredibly red lips.

But to become a professional cartoonist, Jeff needed a *syndicate*. That's a company that sells comic strips to newspapers all over the United States. The trouble was, no syndicate liked *Igdoof*.

The rejection letters began piling up. One thing became clear to Jeff. His illustrations weren't good enough. They didn't look as professional as the artwork in *Calvin and Hobbes*, *The Far Side*, and other comic strips in the big newspapers. Jeff's drawings looked more like the doodles of a kid in middle school. Even so, Jeff knew he had funny ideas. He just needed a way to share them with an audience, the way he had in college.

Jeff got an idea that might work. What if he wrote an illustrated journal from the point of view of a middle-school kid? Then his drawings wouldn't have to be all that good.

That idea was the beginning of *Diary of a Wimpy Kid*, one of the most popular children's books ever.

COMICS: NOT JUST FOR LAUGHS

COMIC STRIPS ARE CALLED "THE FUNNIES" FOR A REASON. USUALLY THEY MAKE PEOPLE LAUGH. *PEANUTS*, *GARFIELD*, AND *FAMILY CIRCUS* ARE ALL COMICS WRITTEN FOR THIS REASON.

BUT SOME COMICS ARE MORE THAN FUNNY PICTURES AND JOKES. POLITICAL CARTOONS MIX HUMOR WITH A MESSAGE. FOR EXAMPLE, IN *DOONESBURY*, GARRY TRUDEAU HUMOROUSLY EXPRESSES HIS OWN VIEWS ON SOCIETY AND EVENTS HAPPENING IN THE REAL WORLD.

Chapter 1
Wimpy Moments

On February 19, 1971, Brian Kinney arrived at
the Malcolm Grow Medical Facility, the hospital
on Andrews Air Force Base in Prince George's
County, Maryland. He got there just minutes after
his wife, Patricia, gave birth to their third child.
He was disappointed that he hadn't been able to
make it in time. But when he saw his newborn son,
Brian felt incredibly proud.

Weighing ten pounds, which is a lot for a newborn, Jeff looked strong and healthy. There was certainly nothing wimpy about him.

Brian was an officer in the United States Navy. Patricia was a full-time mother. After leaving the hospital, the Kinneys brought Jeff to their home in Upper Marlboro, Maryland. There, Jeff met his older sister and brother— Annmarie and Scott—for the first time. Scott, who was only three at the time, thought that Jeff 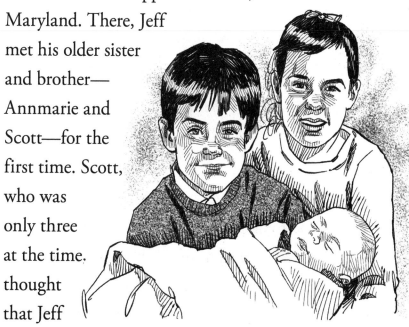 was cute. "He's a doorbell," he said. He meant to say *adorable*.

But being a younger brother was sometimes hard. As Jeff got a little older, Annmarie and Scott played pranks on him. On the first day of summer vacation one year, Scott woke Jeff up very early. Jeff was only about seven years old. Scott told him to get ready for school. He said that Jeff had slept through the entire vacation.

He'd even missed the family's trip to Disney World! Jeff got up and rushed to get dressed for school. It took several minutes before he realized it was a joke.

The family moved to Fort Washington, Maryland, when Jeff was three. Not long after, in 1976, there was happy news. Patrick Kinney was born. Finally, Jeff had a little brother. He wasn't the youngest or smallest Kinney kid.

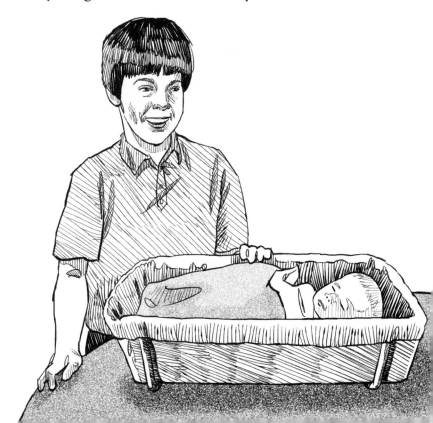

Jeff was good at being a big brother. He'd build mazes out of pillows and blankets for Patrick to crawl through. On hot summer nights, the brothers often slept in the cool basement. Patrick would lie awake listening to his big brother tell jokes and make up funny stories. Often, they'd laugh so much that their dad would come downstairs and yell at them to knock it off and go to sleep.

Although Jeff enjoyed having an audience, sometimes his little brother was a pain in the neck. Patrick, Jeff thought, was spoiled. He never got punished. Once, Patrick drew a life-size drawing of himself in permanent marker on the pantry door in the kitchen. Jeff couldn't wait for his parents to see it. He was sure Patrick would be in big trouble. Instead, Brian and Patricia loved it!

They never painted over it. Years later, when the house was sold, the drawing was still there. To Jeff, this seemed completely unfair. If he'd done the same thing, he would have been punished.

Jeff was learning that childhood has its ups and downs, especially when you're one of four kids. For this reason, he liked the novels of Judy Blume. Here was an author who wrote about problems Jeff experienced in his own life. Like having a pesky younger brother. Always an avid reader, Jeff admired how Judy Blume used humor to describe real-life situations.

JUDY BLUME

Jeff learned to love reading from his dad. Brian Kinney had a drawer filled with comic books. The copies of *Uncle Scrooge* by Carl Barks were Jeff's favorite. These comic books taught Jeff a lot about what makes good storytelling and comedy.

Jeff's dad also enjoyed the morning funnies and passed this love on to his children. Each day, they'd wake up to find that their father had left the *Washington Post* open to the comics page. Often, if there

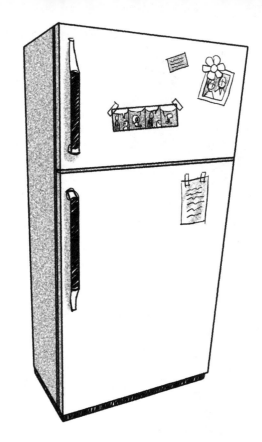

was a strip he really wanted everyone to see, Mr. Kinney cut it out and put it on the refrigerator.

Jeff's childhood was a great time for comics. He admired the excellent cartoonists that gave his family so many laughs. *Calvin and Hobbes* by Bill Watterson was one of those comic strips.

It was about an unruly first-grader named Calvin, and his pal, Hobbes, a tiger. In the strip, everybody except Calvin sees Hobbes as a stuffed animal. But to Calvin, he is real.

BILL WATTERSON

Along with *Calvin and Hobbes*, *Bloom County* and *The Far Side* made up the "holy trinity of cartoons" for Jeff. The Kinney family bought collections of these comics and read them over and over again. Today, these books are ragged from so many years of use and enjoyment.

Even as a kid Jeff loved to draw, just like the cartoonists his dad introduced him to.

At Potomac Landing Elementary School, Jeff's favorite subject was art. And even when he wasn't in art class, he liked to draw in his many sketch pads. Everyone thought Jeff was very talented. That made him feel proud. But his fifth-grade teacher, Mrs. Norton, offered Jeff advice on ways to make his drawings even better.

Jeff was used to people praising his sketches. It surprised him when Mrs. Norton didn't do the same. Still, he listened to what she had to say. Because of Mrs. Norton, over time, Jeff's drawings got better.

Mrs. Norton also changed the way Jeff looked at comedy. Once, Jeff and his friends were practicing for the school talent show. Mrs. Norton walked into the room. She found Jeff and the other boys wriggling around inside a bunch of sheets that had been sewn together.

The boys were supposed to be a giant snake. They thought it was hilarious, but their act really wasn't very funny. Mrs. Norton gently said that there was a difference between people laughing *with* you and people laughing *at* you. Jeff understood what she meant: Just looking foolish wasn't real comedy.

Jeff learned that humor came from paying attention to the world around him. One day, this skill would help him create the world of Greg Heffley, the main character of *Diary of a Wimpy Kid*. "I was never the best student or the best athlete, but I was always an observer," Jeff has said. "I never felt like a participant. I just quietly watched and listened to what was going on around me."

Although he may have felt like an outsider, Jeff had plenty of friends. He liked the same things as many other kids, like playing sports. Often, though, he found clever ways to get out of team practices. Swim practices, he remembers, weren't fun. They were early in the morning and very tiring. But Jeff realized that there was no way his coach could keep track of every kid on the team. So he'd ask to go to the bathroom.

He'd hide there until practice was over. However, the bathroom was very cold. And Jeff was dripping wet after coming out of the pool. He had to find a way to keep warm. The answer was to wrap himself in toilet paper and sit on the toilet until practice was over. "I wouldn't say I was a wimpy kid," Jeff has said, "but I definitely had my wimpy moments."

JUDY BLUME

JUDY BLUME'S *TALES OF A FOURTH GRADE NOTHING* WAS JEFF'S FAVORITE BOOK AS A CHILD. IT TOLD THE STORY OF PETER HATCHER. LIFE WAS FRUSTRATING TO PETER, MAINLY BECAUSE OF HIS LITTLE BROTHER, FUDGE. FUDGE CUTS HIS OWN HAIR, THROWS TEMPER TANTRUMS, AND EVEN EATS PETER'S PET TURTLE! INSTEAD OF GETTING IN TROUBLE, THOUGH, FUDGE ALMOST NEVER GETS PUNISHED.

THE CHARACTER WAS SO POPULAR THAT JUDY BLUME CREATED FOUR MORE BOOKS ABOUT FUDGE AND THE HATCHER FAMILY.

OTHER POPULAR JUDY BLUME BOOKS INCLUDE *FRECKLE JUICE*; *BLUBBER*; AND *ARE YOU THERE GOD? IT'S ME, MARGARET*. TODAY, JEFF KINNEY TRIES TO WRITE IN AN EQUALLY REALISTIC WAY. HE HOPES THAT HIS READERS CAN IDENTIFY WITH GREG HEFFLEY, JUST AS HE DID WITH PETER HATCHER.

Chapter 2
A Tough Decision

To Greg Heffley, middle school is a weird
place. There are kids who haven't yet hit their
growth spurt. They are mixed in with giants
twice their size who are already shaving! Middle
school at Eugene Burroughs in Accokeek,
Maryland, seemed pretty strange to Jeff. Like
Greg, Jeff wasn't the smallest or the biggest
kid in the class. He was just somewhere in the
middle.

What set him apart from his classmates was
his artwork. By this time, it was getting quite
good. It was so good, in fact, that Jeff's teachers
thought everyone should see it. They asked Jeff
to keep some of his best drawings in the display
case in the lobby.

Patrick, Jeff's little brother, wanted people to admire Jeff's drawings, too. He knew his friends would be really impressed by Jeff's pictures of Star Wars characters. Without asking, Patrick took one of Jeff's sketchbooks to school.

Patrick was right. Jeff's classmates liked the drawings a lot. In fact, they offered to buy them. That was fine with Patrick. When Jeff found out that Patrick had sold his drawings, he was furious!

In middle school, Jeff discovered a new interest. It was one that would change his life. One day in 1985, Jeff's mom bought a home computer. It was made by a new company called Apple. The Kinneys, like most other families at that time, had never owned a computer.

Most people were happy just using their computers to write papers or play games. Not Jeff. He wanted to know how the computer actually worked. He began learning to write his own games. Using books and magazines, he taught himself how to be a computer programmer.

It was hard for his parents to keep him away from his new hobby. Once, when Jeff got in trouble, Brian and Patricia told him he couldn't use the computer to write his programs.

That wasn't going to stop Jeff. He hid in his room and wrote his programs by hand on a sheet of paper. Today, Jeff laughs at this memory. This was the most rebellious thing he ever did in middle school.

Jeff's interest in computers continued in high school at Bishop McNamara in Forestville, Maryland. In fact, one summer, the University of Maryland hired him to develop a computer program. This was an important experience for Jeff. He saw that his understanding of computers was a valuable skill. One day this skill might even lead to a job.

LIFE BEFORE HOME COMPUTERS

BEFORE THE 1980S, MOST FAMILIES DIDN'T OWN A COMPUTER. SO IF YOUR TEACHER ASKED YOU TO WRITE A REPORT, YOU HAD TO GO TO THE LIBRARY TO FIND THE INFORMATION YOU NEEDED. THEN YOU HAD TO WRITE YOUR PAPER BY HAND OR USE A TYPEWRITER. EITHER WAY, SCHOOLWORK TOOK A LOT LONGER TO COMPLETE. IF YOU MADE A MISTAKE ON A HANDWRITTEN REPORT, YOU MIGHT HAVE TO START IT ALL OVER!

THE FIRST GAMING CONSOLES DIDN'T BECOME POPULAR UNTIL THE EARLY 1980S. BEFORE THAT, KIDS LIKE JEFF FLOCKED TO ARCADES. THERE, THEY HAD TO PAY MONEY, USUALLY TWENTY-FIVE CENTS, FOR EVERY GAME THEY PLAYED.

WHEN APPLE, IBM, AND OTHER COMPANIES BEGAN MAKING AFFORDABLE HOME COMPUTERS, THE WORLD CHANGED. DOING SCHOOLWORK AND PLAYING GAMES BECAME MUCH EASIER. AND WHEN THE INTERNET TOOK OFF IN THE LATE 1990S, PEOPLE SUDDENLY HAD INSTANT ACCESS TO MORE INFORMATION THAN THEY COULD FIND IN ANY LIBRARY!

Jeff enjoyed high school. He really liked
English classes, and his interest in art remained
strong. Jeff's grades were so good that he ended
up graduating third in his class.

That didn't mean life was always easy for
him. In some ways, Jeff continued to feel like an
outsider, an observer. For instance, at McNamara,

he was on the soccer team. Jeff thought sports should be fun. The coach, however, yelled a lot and punished his players. If they made mistakes or didn't obey, he'd make them run sprints. Jeff didn't understand why his coach was so mean. Once, while Jeff and some of the other boys were getting water, the coach yelled, "Get your butts over here!" Jeff thought it would be funny to do exactly what his coach said. He ran toward his coach backward, with his rear end sticking up in the air. His coach

didn't think it was funny at all. Jeff realized that he wasn't a good fit for the team and quit playing soccer.

In his senior year, Jeff had to make an important decision. What university would he attend? His grades were excellent, so he could choose from some of the best schools in the country. But college is very expensive, and Jeff's parents weren't rich. The United States Air Force offered Jeff a full scholarship to Villanova University in Pennsylvania. That meant Jeff could go there for free.

VILLANOVA
UNIVERSITY

Jeff's decision was easy. He said yes.

The US military often pays for bright students to go to college. In return, the students must receive special training and also promise to stay in the military for a number of years after college. In Jeff's case, it would mean joining the air force.

Villanova is several hours away from Maryland. Even though he was far from home, Jeff enjoyed it and became involved in campus life. He wanted to join the staff of the campus newspaper. What he hoped to do was write crossword puzzles. But the editor wasn't looking for a crossword-puzzle writer. He asked Jeff if he had any other ideas. "Maybe I could write a cartoon," Jeff suggested. The editor liked that idea.

Even though he had never been a cartoonist, Jeff found it easy to come up with material. Igdoof was the main character and the title of the strip.

He was a freshman in college, just like Jeff. And also like Jeff, Igdoof had to deal with making it to class on time, studying for exams, and living with a roommate.

Jeff loved being a campus cartoonist. But he realized that he wasn't suited for a career in the air force. Instead, he wanted a job where he could be creative and make people laugh. So he made a very difficult decision. He decided to give up his scholarship to Villanova. That meant switching to a school that wasn't so expensive. Jeff moved closer to home and attended the University of Maryland, where he hoped Igdoof could live on.

Chapter 3
A Big Idea

Jeff quickly found a new home at the University of Maryland, but Igdoof didn't. For over a year, Jeff tried unsuccessfully to get his cartoon in the school's newspaper called the *Diamondback*. The paper was known for having some of the most talented college cartoonists in the country. Jeff was up against stiff competition.

Finally, Jeff received the phone call he'd been waiting for: One of the paper's three cartoonists had decided to quit.

If Jeff still wanted to do a cartoon, the slot was his!

Igdoof was an instant hit. Thousands of college students read the strip every day. Once, Igdoof showed up to class in his pajamas. Another time, he covered himself in chocolate syrup. With huge ears and a giant nose, Igdoof even *looked* funny. The comic was so popular that other colleges on the East Coast picked it up and put it in their newspapers.

Igdoof wanted to be a college cartoonist, just like Jeff. In some of the cartoons, Igdoof is shown making his own comics, like *Manny the Talking Sideburn*. Sometimes he'd make himself a character in one of his own comics. Igdoof's pictures of himself show a guy with small ears and a normal-size nose. This was how Igdoof saw himself. Examining them closely, these pictures look a lot like the character that would one day become Greg Heffley.

For Jeff, being a popular cartoonist was a dream come true. In the mornings, he loved going into the dining hall and watching other students as they read that day's strip.

Jeff knew that he wanted a future in cartooning. So he began writing letters to professional cartoonists, asking for advice. One was Lincoln

Peirce, who wrote a strip called *Big Nate*. The cartoon is about a sixth-grader named Nate Wright. Jeff was a fan of the comic and followed Nate's adventures in the *Washington Post* newspaper. Mr. Peirce really liked Jeff's work. He gave him lots of tips. One suggestion was to avoid cramming too much into word bubbles.

LINCOLN PEIRCE

Jeff had no idea what his new friend would do next. One Sunday, Jeff opened up the *Washington Post* to read the comics. He couldn't believe what he saw. There, in that day's *Big Nate*,

was a drawing of Nate's school notebook. It was covered in stickers. Along with Bart Simpson and Garfield was a sticker of Igdoof. A drawing of Jeff's character was in the *Washington Post*! He wouldn't forget Lincoln Peirce's kind gesture.

Jeff enjoyed the attention that came from having a popular cartoon, but inventing a brand-new comic every day, five days a week, wasn't easy. First, he had to think of a funny idea. That was usually the hardest part. Then, Jeff had to draw the cartoon in pencil before inking it with a pen. Each strip had four panels, so working on *Igdoof* would often keep Jeff up all night. That didn't leave him much time for sleep or schoolwork.

Although it was a struggle to balance doing a daily comic strip with college courses, Jeff managed to graduate in 1993. By that time, Jeff had written nearly three hundred comic strips. He put them all together in *Igdoof Bathroom Companion*, his very first book. Jeff quickly sold every copy and even had a book signing at the university bookstore.

After graduation, Jeff began mailing samples of his work to every cartoon syndicate in the country. While he waited for their responses, his life after college began taking shape. In 1995, Jeff got married and moved to Massachusetts. That's where his wife, Nicole, would be attending law school. To make money, Jeff first got a job as a graphic designer for a newspaper called the *Newburyport Daily News*.

Jeff then began working for a company called UpToDate. He helped develop computer software that doctors used to make good decisions when treating their patients.

Even though it wasn't his dream job, Jeff enjoyed working at UpToDate. He especially loved playing pranks on his coworkers. He often called up his friends at the company and pretended to be a confused customer.

To have some fun and serve his community,
too, he signed up for Big Brothers Big Sisters. This
is a program that places boys and girls with an
adult role model. Jeff and his "little brother" did a
lot of fun things together, like play video games
and go on outdoor adventures. Jeff always tried to

use his humor to bring a smile to his little brother's face. But lots of times it was the little brother who made Jeff laugh. Once, after a long day of having fun, Jeff said to his little brother, "You pooped?" The little brother didn't understand that Jeff was asking him if he was tired. He wrinkled up his face and said, "No!" Jeff cracked up.

Sadly for Jeff and Nicole, their marriage wasn't working out. In 1998, they got a divorce. Also, Jeff had heard back from the cartoon syndicates and the news was disappointing. They weren't interested in his comic.

Being alone again wasn't easy. Jeff considered moving closer to his family, who now lived in Virginia. But if he left Massachusetts, he knew he'd have to leave his little brother behind. And he didn't want to do that. Also, he thought, he'd feel like a failure if he moved home. His marriage had ended and he still wasn't a cartoonist. So he decided to stay where he was and rebuild his life.

As a way to stay focused on his cartooning, Jeff began keeping a journal. He wrote down everything.

He also included funny stories about things that happened during the day. Between the lines of text, he'd often draw little doodles to illustrate some of these funny stories. That's when he came up with a big idea.

Many of the rejection letters from the cartoon syndicates told Jeff that his artwork needed to look more professional. In his journal, his doodles were very simple. They looked a lot like the drawings many kids keep in their school notebooks.

Suddenly, he realized he had a great idea for a book. He'd write a journal from the point of view of a child and illustrate it with simple drawings, just as a kid might do. He even knew what kind of child he'd be writing about. He'd call it *Diary of a Wimpy Kid*.

Jeff was excited. He couldn't wait to get started. But he remembered some advice from Mrs. Norton, his elementary school teacher. She once told him that before starting a project, he should make a plan. So Jeff decided not to jump right into writing. Instead, he bought a notebook. He planned to fill it with every funny experience and idea he could think of. Only after the notebook was completely filled would he actually begin to write the book.

Jeff figured it would take him a month, maybe two, to fill up his ideas notebook. Instead, it took him four years.

Chapter 4
Greg Heffley in the Big Apple

By the time Jeff was finished with his ideas notebook, he had seventy-seven pages of characters, jokes, and story ideas. The pages were jam-packed with material. You practically needed a microscope to read them. All of this was good. It meant that Jeff had plenty of ideas to start his book.

In Jeff's mind, *Diary of a Wimpy Kid* would be a very long book, somewhere between seven hundred and thirteen hundred pages! He imagined it would be for adults who'd enjoy being reminded of what it was like to be a kid. Not once did Jeff think that he was writing a children's book.

Because his dad loved comics so much, Jeff had grown up believing that comics were more for adults than kids. He thought that reading the morning comics was an adult activity that he was allowed to enjoy as well. This had a big impact on Jeff as he wrote *Diary of a Wimpy Kid* and tried to figure out who his audience would be.

During the four years he spent working on his ideas notebook, Jeff's life changed in two important ways. First, in 1999, he got a new job developing online games for a company called Pearson Education. It owned a website called Funbrain. Here, Jeff created fun and silly games to help kids learn. In Ball Hogs, one of those games, kids tested their math skills as tennis ball–fetching pigs.

NOT JUST FOR KIDS

THE FAR SIDE BY GARY LARSON WAS A POPULAR SINGLE-PANEL COMIC IN THE 1980S AND 1990S. LARSON WAS KNOWN FOR HIS BIZARRE SENSE OF HUMOR AND INTEREST IN THE NATURAL WORLD. MANY OF HIS CARTOONS WERE ABOUT ANIMALS BEHAVING A LOT LIKE HUMANS.

BERKELEY BREATHED'S *BLOOM COUNTY* WAS ABOUT AN ODD CAST OF CHARACTERS THAT LIVED IN A SMALL AMERICAN TOWN. POLITICS AND SOCIAL ISSUES WERE THE SUBJECTS OF MANY OF BREATHED'S STRIPS.

The second big event happened at a friend's dinner party, where Jeff met a woman named Julie Cullinane. They soon started dating and in 2000, they got married and moved to a little house in the town of Plainville, Massachusetts. There, they had their first child, Will, in 2002. Grant, their second son, would follow in 2005.

After work every day, Jeff would go to his
basement to write. Jeff wanted to use only the
best ideas from his notebook. Deciding what was
funny took a long time. After spending four years
just writing down his ideas, he now spent four
more years writing the first draft of his book.

As he worked on that draft, his characters
began to take shape. In some ways, the Heffley
family was a lot like Jeff's family growing up.

Both had a dad who was interested in the Civil War, and a teenage son who played drums in a rock band. But the Heffley family was more like a funhouse-mirror version of the Kinneys, where everyone's personality was exaggerated. Greg himself was becoming an exaggerated version of what Jeff says were his worst qualities as a kid. The childhood moments when Jeff acted selfishly or foolishly all helped make Greg the believable character he became.

Other characters were purely fictional. A not-always-nice character like Greg needs a best friend who is his complete opposite. That's how Jeff came up with Greg's loyal and kind pal, Rowley Jefferson. Fregley, Greg's oddball neighbor, is also totally made up. Jeff says that everyone knows a kid like Fregley. And if you don't, then *you* might actually be Fregley.

Working on *Diary of a Wimpy Kid* wasn't always fun. Jeff's basement office was very cold

and damp. Often, he'd go downstairs to write
and find that rain or snow had flooded the space.

On those miserable days, he'd wonder if all his
hard work would pay off. But he had a dream and
was willing to work hard. One day, he hoped he

could walk into a store and point to his book on the shelf, saying, "I wrote that."

Jeff wasn't the only one who hoped that *Diary of a Wimpy Kid* would eventually get published. His family and friends knew how funny his ideas and drawings were. They thought that other people would like them, too. Jess Brallier, Jeff's boss, was one of those early fans of *Diary of a Wimpy Kid*. So when Jeff suggested offering bits of his book on Funbrain, Jess agreed.

JESS BRALLIER

This was an interesting experiment. There were other comic strips online, but many people didn't believe that a Web comic could be very successful.

Still, Jeff thought that it might work. If he posted one entry from Greg's journal each day, maybe people would read it. And if they did, maybe that would interest a publishing company, which could make it into a real book.

Jeff turned out to be right. Kids and adults from all over the world were logging in on Funbrain each day to read Greg Heffley's latest journal entry. Many of those millions of readers would e-mail questions to Jeff or tell him how funny his stories were. He was thrilled to know that he had fans in such faraway places as Japan and Saudi Arabia.

Then, in 2006, Jess Brallier suggested that Jeff travel to New York City and attend Comic Con. This is a huge gathering of people involved in comic books. There, Jess thought, Jeff might meet someone interested in making a book out of *Diary of a Wimpy Kid*.

It started off as a very discouraging trip.

On the first day of the convention, Jeff wasn't
allowed in the building because it was too full.
On the second day, Jeff walked the aisles with
a sample of his book in hand. He stopped
to show it to every book publisher he
came across. No one seemed
interested at all.

This was like looking for a syndicate for *Igdoof.* Jeff was just about to give up and go home. Then he saw a booth in the last aisle of the convention center. The sign behind the booth read ABRAMS. Earlier in the day, Jeff had heard that Abrams was a publishing company that had recently turned a Web comic into a book.

Nervously, Jeff approached the man at the booth. Jeff asked him if he'd like to see a sample of his work. The man, who introduced himself as Charles Kochman, agreed to look at it. After flipping through the pages for about thirty seconds, Charles looked at Jeff and said, "This is exactly what we're looking for." After the convention,

Charles took Jeff's samples to his editorial team at Abrams. Everyone thought that they were perfect.

Jeff was overjoyed. After spending eight years creating *Diary of a Wimpy Kid*, he'd found a publisher. Not only that, but Abrams said it wanted a series, not just one book. A whole series! This was music to Jeff's ears. However, what he heard next caught him by surprise. Abrams wanted *Diary of a Wimpy Kid* to be a children's book. All this time, Jeff thought he was writing for adults!

Charlie and Abrams had their reasons for aiming Jeff's book at kids. For a long time, many publishers believed that boys didn't like to read. Abrams was hoping that *Diary of a Wimpy Kid* could change that. According to Charles, boys will read "if you give them something they *want* to read." He knew that Jeff's work looked like something he would have wanted to read when he was a kid.

Charles became Jeff's editor. Over the next

several months, they worked together to develop the first book of the series. There was a lot of work to do. Jeff originally planned to make one giant book. He now had to take his 1,300-page manuscript and turn it into a single 224-page volume.

In 2007, *Diary of a Wimpy Kid* was released. No one knew if anyone would actually buy it, and at first, things didn't look good. At a public event to celebrate the book, Jeff's family and his editor's friends were the only people who showed up.

But it wouldn't take long for things to change in a big way. People—kids—were buying the book! A month after its release, Jeff got exciting news. *Diary of a Wimpy Kid* had made the *New York Times* Best Seller list. This meant that it was one of the most popular books in the country. It looked like Jeff's dream was coming true!

CHARLES KOCHMAN

IF NOT FOR CHARLES KOCHMAN, MILLIONS OF PEOPLE MAY HAVE NEVER HEARD OF GREG HEFFLEY.

"CHARLIE" HAD YEARS OF EXPERIENCE IN THE PUBLISHING INDUSTRY. HE WORKED ON MANY ILLUSTRATED TITLES, INCLUDING *MAD MAGAZINE*,

SUPERMAN AND BATMAN COMIC BOOKS, AND THE CHOOSE YOUR OWN ADVENTURE SERIES. HE KNEW WHAT KIDS LIKED TO READ AND THOUGHT THEY WOULD ENJOY JEFF'S BOOK, TOO. SHORTLY AFTER MEETING JEFF, CHARLIE MADE IT HIS MISSION TO MAKE SURE *DIARY OF A WIMPY KID* GOT PUBLISHED.

CHARLIE THOUGHT THE SIMPLE DRAWINGS WERE PERFECT. WITH GREG'S KIDLIKE VOICE, THESE DRAWINGS HELPED MAKE *DIARY OF A WIMPY KID* SEEM LIKE IT REALLY WAS WRITTEN BY A BOY IN JUNIOR HIGH.

SINCE THEIR FIRST MEETING, CHARLIE HAS WORKED CLOSELY WITH JEFF. AS JEFF'S EDITOR, HE IS RESPONSIBLE FOR READING EACH DRAFT AND PROVIDING FEEDBACK TO MAKE EACH BOOK BETTER. SOMETIMES HE HELPS JEFF IMPROVE HIS STORIES. OTHER TIMES HE LETS JEFF KNOW IF HE THINKS A JOKE IS FUNNY OR NOT. JEFF KNOWS HOW IMPORTANT CHARLIE HAS BEEN TO HIS CAREER AND EVEN THANKED HIM IN A SPECIAL WAY. *HARD LUCK*, THE EIGHTH BOOK IN THE SERIES, IS DEDICATED TO CHARLIE.

Chapter 5
Flying High

The success of Jeff's first book was just the beginning. The series became more popular as time went on and new *Wimpy Kid* books came out.

Diary of a Wimpy Kid was proving to be very popular in other countries as well as the United States. Many teachers and parents began writing about the book online and sending Jeff letters. He started to notice a certain phrase appearing over and over again. That phrase was "reluctant reader." At first, Jeff didn't know what it meant. But he soon discovered that there were a lot of kids who didn't like to read at all. Now their teachers and parents were writing to tell Jeff that these same kids couldn't put his book down.

Some other adults were uncomfortable with Greg's behavior. They worried that kids might think it was okay to lie or act selfishly, like Greg. But most people understood that the books were funny *because* of Greg's mistakes. And many kids were learning that reading can be fun. Jeff was happy to know that his book was introducing so many children to a world of reading. He hoped that *Diary of a Wimpy Kid* would make these kids interested in other books as well.

When *Wimpy Kid*'s sequel, *Rodrick Rules*, was released in 2008, it also became a *New York Times* Best Seller. *The Last Straw*, Jeff's third book, did even better. It topped Stephenie Meyer's Twilight series about teenage vampires to become the overall highest-selling book in the country.

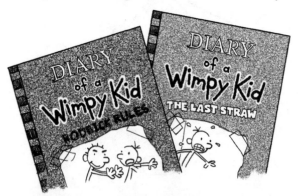

Jeff, whose greatest dream was to get his book published, wasn't just a successful author. He was becoming one of the most successful children's authors in history.

So much of Jeff's success was due to word of mouth. A kid would read *Diary of a Wimpy Kid* and tell his or her friends about it. Then those friends would read it, too. But now adults were taking notice as well. In 2009, Jeff was included in *Time* magazine's list of the 100 Most Influential People.

Jeff still saw himself as a failed cartoonist, so it was strange to be on a list with such famous people as President Barack Obama and Oprah Winfrey. When he and Julie went to a fancy party for all the people who were named to the list that year, they felt very out of place to be around so many celebrities.

The movie industry in Hollywood, California, was also noticing the popularity of Jeff's books. Producers at Twentieth Century Fox thought Greg Heffley deserved to be on the silver screen. However, Fox didn't want to make a movie-length cartoon. Instead, the film company wanted to make a live-action movie. That means filming real people. It was going to be a challenge to turn Jeff's simple drawings into a live-action film. However, Jeff thought that the producers found the perfect kids to play the parts of Greg and his friend Rowley.

MEET THE ACTORS

ZACHARY GORDON WAS LIVING IN LOS ANGELES, WHERE HE WAS ACTING AND GOING TO SCHOOL. HIS ELEVENTH-BIRTHDAY WISH CAME TRUE WHEN HE WAS CAST AS GREG HEFFLEY IN *DIARY OF A WIMPY KID*. UNTIL THEN, HE'D HAD ONLY SMALL PARTS IN TELEVISION AND FILM. THIS WOULD BE HIS BIGGEST ROLE YET.

ZACHARY GORDON

ROBERT CAPRON LIVED IN RHODE ISLAND, ON THE OTHER SIDE OF THE COUNTRY. HE'D ALSO WORKED IN FILM, AND ONSTAGE, TOO. THE PRODUCERS THOUGHT THAT HE WAS PERFECT TO PLAY THE PART OF ROWLEY JEFFERSON, GREG'S KINDHEARTED SIDEKICK.

STARRING IN THREE *WIMPY KID* MOVIES WAS A BIG STEP IN THE BOYS' CAREERS. IT OPENED THE DOOR FOR OTHER ROLES. ROBERT PLAYED THE PART OF YOUNG CURLY IN *THE THREE STOOGES* MOVIE AND DID THE VOICE OF BOB IN THE ANIMATED FILM *FRANKENWEENIE*. ZACHARY

CONTINUES TO ACT IN TELEVISION AND FILM, AND WAS EVEN INTERVIEWED ON *THE TONIGHT SHOW*.

ZACHARY AND ROBERT BECAME GOOD FRIENDS WHILE WORKING TOGETHER ON THE *WIMPY KID* FILMS. THE BOYS AND THEIR FAMILIES ALSO BECAME CLOSE WITH JEFF. ON TWO DIFFERENT BOOK TOURS, THE BOYS AND THEIR PARENTS JOINED JEFF. THEY SURPRISED HIS FANS, WHO DIDN'T KNOW THAT THEY'D ALSO BE MEETING THE STARS OF THE MOVIES!

ROBERT CAPRON

Having his book made into a movie was a new experience for Jeff. During filming, he visited the movie set many times. He sometimes gave ideas to the director and the producers. But most of all, he learned a lot about filmmaking. Jeff found it all so interesting that he decided to write a book about it called *The Wimpy Kid Movie Diary: How Greg Heffley Went Hollywood*.

In its very first weekend, the movie version of *Diary of a Wimpy Kid* made over $22 million! The movie was so successful that two more films followed—*Rodrick Rules* and *Dog Days*, which was based on Jeff's fourth book.

Even though Jeff could walk down the street without being recognized, Greg Heffley was a star. The organizers of the Macy's Thanksgiving Day Parade certainly thought so. In 2010, they added a giant balloon of Greg Heffley to their event. Greg isn't very big for his age, but his balloon is huge. It's as tall as a five-story building and as wide as five taxicabs. Seeing his character flying above the streets of New York City was very special for Jeff. This was the same parade that had included balloons of Bart Simpson and Garfield. These were the same characters that appeared next to Igdoof in the *Big Nate* comic so many years earlier. Now, Greg Heffley was joining them.

The adults who make magazines, movies, and parades had given *Diary of a Wimpy Kid* some very special attention. Still, Jeff's most devoted fans have always been kids. So Jeff was honored when they voted to make *Diary of a Wimpy Kid* their favorite book in the Nickelodeon Kids' Choice

Awards four times. Jeff and his sons even got to attend the ceremony one year.

Even though the awards were nice, the most important thing for Jeff had always been to write funny books that his fans would like. So he continued writing. In 2010, he released his fifth book, *The Ugly Truth*. It was followed by *Cabin Fever* in 2011. Jeff's seventh book, *The Third Wheel*, came out in 2012, and *Hard Luck* debuted in 2013.

As each new book has been released, Jeff has toured different parts of the United States and the rest of the world. At these events at schools and bookstores, Jeff tells his story, signs books, and answers questions from the audience.

Often, these questions are about the color of the next book or how he thought of the names for his characters. But one question that comes up again and again has to do with Greg's age. They wonder if Greg will ever grow up and move on to high school. Jeff doesn't think so. Instead, like so many of his favorite cartoon characters, he says, Greg isn't meant to grow up. So the struggles of being in middle school, dealing with friends, and living in the Heffley household will continue. Greg will forever be a wimpy kid.

FOREIGN EDITIONS

THE DIARY OF A WIMPY KID BOOKS ARE PRINTED IN FORTY-FIVE DIFFERENT LANGUAGES. SOMETIMES, ENGLISH WORDS DON'T EXACTLY TRANSLATE TO THOSE LANGUAGES. THE TRANSLATION OF THE GERMAN EDITION IS *GREG'S JOURNAL: I'M SURROUNDED BY IDIOTS*. IN GERMANY, THE PUBLISHER EXPLAINED, THERE'S NO WORD FOR *WIMPY*. IN BRAZIL, THE TITLE IS *DIÁRIO DE UM BANANA*. JEFF WAS EXCITED WHEN HE SAW THIS. HE WANTED TO KNOW WHAT IT MEANT.

"WHAT DOES *BANANA* MEAN?" HE ASKED.

"IT MEANS *BANANA*," HE WAS TOLD.

Chapter 6
The Balancing Act

Jeff has become more successful than he ever could have expected. He's sold over 150 million books and has fans worldwide. Being a famous author, though, comes with its own set of challenges.

Writing a new book each year isn't easy. It takes a lot of time to think of enough funny ideas to make a good story.

Sometimes Jeff will spend an entire day without thinking of a single joke. On days like these, he worries and wonders how he's going to write another book kids will enjoy. Drawing each picture takes a lot of time, too. Jeff worked for seventeen hours a day on his drawings for his seventh book, *The Third Wheel*. By the time he was done, his hand was so cramped that he could barely hold a pen!

The work almost never stops for Jeff, even when he's on vacation. On family trips, he often has to write and draw for several hours each day. Sometimes this means finding a quiet place to work while everyone else is having fun.

But being away from home is what's hardest for Jeff. Book tours, meetings with people in Hollywood, and visits to the movie set all keep Jeff on the road for days or weeks at a time. During these trips, Jeff misses seeing Julie, Will, and Grant.

Many times, Jeff has taken overnight flights from the West Coast just to make it home in time to coach his boys' basketball or soccer games, or to lead their Cub Scout meetings. He understands that success can make life complicated, so he tries his best to give his family a life that's as ordinary as possible.

This wish for a normal life is one of the reasons Jeff still has a day job. It might surprise some people, but in addition to being such a successful children's author, Jeff continues to work with Jess Brallier, creating a virtual world for kids called Poptropica.

Jeff's busy work schedule doesn't leave much time to relax. But when he has some time off, he spends it with his family. He especially likes taking his wife and kids to watch their two favorite sports teams, the New England Patriots and the Boston Celtics. His family has season tickets to the Celtics. That means they can go to every basketball game if they want. Jeff's sons are crazy about sports and know almost everything about the NBA. Jeff often plays a game with them where he names a player and the boys have to say what his jersey number is. Even when he names a player most people have never heard of, Jeff rarely stumps Will and Grant!

When they get some time alone, Jeff and Julie
enjoy catching up on their favorite television shows
or going to the movies. They also like spending
time with their friends. They often have their
neighbors over for karaoke. Jeff loves singing

songs by his favorite artists, including Bon Jovi and Elton John. He enjoys singing so much that he even figured out a way to do karaoke in his shower. He does that by himself, though—not with his friends!

POPTROPICA

KIDS WHO PLAY ON POPTROPICA VISIT DIFFERENT "ISLANDS," WHERE THEY CARRY OUT ADVENTURES BY PLAYING GAMES AND SOLVING PUZZLES.

EACH ISLAND IS DIFFERENT. IN CRYPTIDS, ONE OF THE MOST POPULAR ISLANDS, THE PLAYER MUST TRAVEL THE WORLD, LOOKING FOR EVIDENCE OF SUCH CREATURES AS THE LOCH NESS MONSTER AND BIGFOOT. KIDS WHO PLAY LUNAR COLONY JOURNEY TO THE MOON, WHERE THEY SEARCH FOR AN ASTRONAUT WHO HAS GONE MISSING. IN MYTHOLOGY ISLAND, PLAYERS SEEK OUT FIVE

SACRED ITEMS FOR THE GREEK GOD ZEUS. OTHER
ISLANDS INCLUDE SUPER POWER ISLAND, SHRINK
RAY ISLAND, AND GAME SHOW ISLAND. THERE ARE
EVEN TWO ISLANDS WITH THE *DIARY OF A WIMPY
KID* CHARACTERS.

WITH OVER HALF A BILLION POPTROPICA
USERS, JEFF HAS PROVEN THAT HIS SUCCESS IS
NOT LIMITED TO *DIARY OF A WIMPY KID*. INSTEAD,
HE'S CREATED A POPULAR VIRTUAL WORLD, WHERE
KIDS GET TO EXPLORE, FIGURE OUT PROBLEMS,
AND HAVE FUN.

Success has meant a lot of hard work and time away from his family. Still, Jeff would not trade it for anything, especially since so much good has come from it. With the money he's made, he's been able to provide a nice life for his family. They moved to a bigger house in Plainville, where they built a swimming pool and a basketball court. Jeff was even able to buy the house next door. He uses it as a home office, where he can work in peace without having to be far from his wife and kids.

Most important, Jeff has tried to use his wealth to help others, including the people of his town. For many years, there was an old building in the center of Plainville. It was falling apart and made the whole town look bad. No one knew what to do. Jeff and his wife realized that they had an opportunity to build a new, beautiful building in its place. They decided to buy it and turn it into something everyone could enjoy. So that's what they did. In 2015, Jeff opened a bookstore called An Unlikely Story. Upstairs is a space for people to have parties and other events. And on the top floor, Jeff has a studio. At certain times, visitors can stop by and see where he works.

Even when there was doubt about whether or not Jeff would succeed, there were many people who believed in him and helped him get started. Lincoln Peirce, the creator of *Big Nate*, was one of those people. Jeff never forgot the kindness the cartoonist showed by including Igdoof in his comic strip. So when Jeff had the chance to return the favor, he did. In 2009, Jeff helped launch Big Nate Island on Poptropica. Although the comic strip had been around for years in newspapers across the United States, many kids had never heard of it. But having its own Poptropica island allowed *Big Nate*'s popularity to boom.

Millions of kids discovered the comic for the
first time, which led to Mr. Peirce's very own
successful book series.

Being able to help a friend like Lincoln Peirce
is just one reason Jeff continues to work so hard.
But keeping his fans happy is his biggest job.
Diary of a Wimpy Kid has shown millions of kids
that reading can be fun.

Jeff also hopes his fans can learn something from his own experiences. He sees himself as an ordinary guy who refused to give up on his dream. When speaking to a high school graduating class, he told the young men and women that there are two things that can make you successful. One is opportunity. The other is hard work. "We can't always control the opportunity. Some people get lucky and some people don't," he said. But, he continued, "Anything worth having is worth working for, and if you put in the time, you'll be ready when you have the opportunity."

ABOUT THE AUTHOR

DID YOU HAPPEN TO NOTICE THE LAST NAME OF THE AUTHOR? IT'S KINNEY—SAME AS JEFF'S. IS THAT A COINCIDENCE?

NO!

PATRICK KINNEY IS THE YOUNGER BROTHER OF JEFF KINNEY. HE LIVES IN VIRGINIA, WHERE HE WORKS AS A WRITER AND A FITNESS INSTRUCTOR. HE'S GROWN NOW, BUT PATRICK STILL LOVES HEARING JEFF'S STORIES—JUST LIKE HE DID ON THOSE HOT SUMMER NIGHTS IN THE KINNEY FAMILY'S BASEMENT.

TIMELINE OF JEFF KINNEY'S LIFE

1971	Jeffrey Patrick Kinney born February 19
1974	Moves with his family to Fort Washington, Maryland
1989	Begins writing *Igdoof* at Villanova University
1990–1993	Attends the University of Maryland Publishes *The Igdoof Bathroom Companion*
1995	Moves to Massachusetts with his first wife
1998	Gets divorced Begins gathering material for *Diary of a Wimpy Kid*
1999	Begins working for Pearson Education
2000	Marries Julie Cullinane
2002	First son, Will Kinney, is born
2004	*Diary of a Wimpy Kid* appears on Funbrain
2005	Grant Kinney is born
2006	Attends Comic Con in New York City and meets Charles Kochman
2007	Publishes *Diary of a Wimpy Kid* Launches first Poptropica island
2009	*The Last Straw* becomes the best-selling book in the United States Jeff named to *Time* magazine's list of 100 Most Influential People
2010	First Diary of a Wimpy Kid movie is released Greg Heffley balloon added to the Macy's Thanksgiving Day Parade
2015	Opens a bookstore and studio in Plainville, Massachusetts

TIMELINE OF THE WORLD

The first e-mail is sent	1971
The first home video game console is released	1972
The first portable cell phone call is made	1973
Pac-Man video game is released	1980
IBM introduces Personal Computers (PCs)	1981
Sally Ride becomes the first American woman in space	1983
The space shuttle *Challenger* explodes	1986
The Hubble Space Telescope goes into orbit	1990
The general public gains access to the World Wide Web	1991
The final *Calvin and Hobbes* comic strip is published	1995
The first Harry Potter book is released in the United Kingdom	1997
Terrorist airplane attacks destroy the World Trade Center in New York City, damage the Pentagon, and result in the deaths of almost 3,000 people	2001
Twilight is published	2005
WikiLeaks, an organization that leaks top secret information to the public on the Web, is founded	2006
Apple releases the iPhone	2007
Barack Obama is the first African American elected president of the United States	2008
Queen Elizabeth II becomes the longest-reigning monarch in British history	2015

LOOK OUT FOR MORE BOOKS IN THE WHO WAS? SERIES!